CW01645665

Soulful Whispers

A RELEASE by Ganiyah Experience

BY

Tope Fajingbesi Balogun

Copyright © 2018 Tope Fajingbesi Balogun

All rights reserved. No part of this publication may be reproduced, stored in a retrieval system, or transmitted, in any form or in any means by electronic, mechanical, photocopying, recording or otherwise without prior written permission.

ISBN: 978-0-9890868-5-1

Release By Ganiyah

When I chose to call my lifes work - RELEASE, I wasnt fully aware of the literal meaning of the word. I was attending Lisa Nichols conference in California when the word came to me, and it just fit the vision I had in my mind, but I couldnt explain it. I wasnt even sure how to articulate it to the ladies I was having lunch with that day.

On February 28, 2018, almost 3 years after choosing to call my work RELEASE, I decided to check the exact meaning of the word, and I am writing this in awe of Gods majesty. According to Webster dictionary, to release means *to allow or enable to escape from confinement; set free* It also defines it as to *allow (something) to move, act, or flow freely*.

My lifes work is to inspire and empower my tribe to find, learn to fund and fully unleash their purpose in the world no matter what. In short, I am here to work and walk with my tribe to escape confinement. Through my programs and publications such as this collection of poetry, quotes and photos, my previous publications (*What Color is Your Money?* and *Love in Cancun*,) She-EO by Ganiyah, RELEASE seminars and future projects God willing, I aspire to do one thing and one thing only - create spaces for my tribe to release the greatness that is already within them by sharing proven tools that enable them to *Review*, *Expel*, *Learn*, *Engage*, *Attract*, *Serve* and*Evolve* - ***RELEASE***.

I believe that time is a more precious resource than money, so I am honored that you have chosen to invest your time in this book and my other programs. I pray that you continue to receive dividends from it. I also hope this book inspires you to invite me to work with you and your tribe of employees, colleagues and members. It will be the honor of my life to serve you.

Thank you very much for reading! May God bless you.

Love,

Tope Fajingbesi Balogun

Ganiyah

www.ganiyah.com

Dedication

To my mom Taiwo M. Fajingbesi, thank you for being an inspiration.

To my dad late Kolawole G. Fajingbesi, thank you for teaching me how to use my wings.

To my husband AbdulKarim Niyi Balogun, thank you for being my proof that God loves me.

And to my nieces and nephews - my cheerleading squad, may you live long and well, and may our expectations regarding you be exceeded.

Appreciation

To Aameenah Yunus-Ali, who made compiling my manuscript one of her accomplishments while on maternity leave.

To Ayobami Olugbenga-Wyse for editing the photos I took with my telephone, and making them book worthy.

To my editors - Maryam Funmilayo and Flora Brown.

And to my tribe. Thank you for believing in my ability to work and walk with you. I hope my words cheer you, make you smile, and remind you that you are loved, and your work is important. I also hope it pushes you to pay attention to your pain so that you will find, and fearlessly pursue exactly what you were put on this earth to do, no matter what.

May God bless you.

If your mind can conceive it,
your Lord can do it.

Every human being has two duties:
To find what they were created to do,
and then find the person(s) created
to help them do it.

Contents

Like Trees

Perhaps we should treat good relationships like trees. After all, we dont chop off the good ones in anger when they are dull and bare in the fall. We leave and love them in spite of their bareness because we remember that the same trees are full of beautiful leaves in the spring, and provide shade and cool breeze in the summer.

- May 14th, 2010

Seize The Power

We lose all opportunities to apologize, appreciate, and achieve when we die, so lets seize this moment, and use the power of NOW, to live our best life today because the next breath is not guaranteed.

- May 18th, 2010

What Type Are You?

There are three types of people: receivers, servers, and pillars. Receivers can accept help and love from others, but are mostly unable to give.

Servers are always there for the people in their lives, but hardly have anyone to turn to when they are in need. Pillars are the best, they are solid rocks to those who need them, and are blessed to have a strong tribe in their time of need as well.

What type are you? And what do you want to be?

- June 3rd, 2010

Stay Alive

The difference between those who live and those who just exist is PASSION. You have to be passionate about something; the thing that keeps you dreaming, hoping, and shaping your world, not the blood flowing through your veins, is what keeps you alive. Without passion, you are a dead man walking.

- June 8th, 2010

Rashidi

We are actors,
And our show times are fixed.
When our time is up,
We must take a bow,
Whether we like it or not.
When I take my final bow,
I pray that the angels and the people testify
That I lived my life with passion,
Loved deeply,
Pursued my calling faithfully,
Fell plenty times,
But always rose with divine strength.

-May 5th, 2012
Dedicated to one of Nigerias finest
- Rashidi Yekini (RIP)

Forgiveness

Forgiving people who hurt, betray, or oppress us is tough and requires a very high altitude of faith, but it is a necessity.

Its like flying a plane in turbulent weather and trying to climb to 34,000 feet; the winds and storms try to keep the plane from ascending, but a good pilot knows that he must keep climbing in order to have a smooth ride.

The key to unlocking forgiveness is knowing that you cannot do it all alone, or for the sake of the oppressor. It can only be done with divine help and the realization that forgiveness is solely for the benefit of your own soul.

- July 11th, 2012

No Shame

Never let anyone make you feel ashamed of your trials; a trial that didnt kill you wasnt meant for you alone, it was brought for you to earn the diploma to teach those struggling behind.

Therefore, you must speak without fear when you get on top of the mountain because your trials make you a victor, not a victim.

- December 17th, 2012

Faith Or Fear (1)

In order to make true progress, faith has to be stronger than fear. Faith that what you are called to do will succeed and sustain you, even when all available physical evidence makes you fear that it cant.

October 10th, 2013

Faith Or Fear (2)

No matter how many options you are presented with, when it comes to making a decision, there are only two real choices - Faith or Fear. Sadly, many of us choose fear over faith and expect miracles. This is true regardless of what the matter comes draped in - whether you are considering marriage, divorce, children, further education, relocation, investment or anything else, remember to choose faith over fear.

- November 24th, 2013

Pain

Pain has purpose
It brings PERSPECTIVE
Teaches PATIENCE
Leads to new PATHS
Weeds out unproductive PEOPLE
Places us in POSITIONS
Opens doors of PLEASURE
And empowers us to PRAY.
But only if we use it, instead of letting it use us.
Are you using your pain?

February 14th, 2014

The Trust

Each moment we are awake, (and) breathing represents a unique opportunity to use the keys to an empire we hold in trust, for good. That empire, my friend, is our time.

- June 25th, 2014

Knock Knock

There is no such thing as overnight success. Success is the magic that happens when you are close to the door when opportunity knocks.

- October 6th, 2014

Spring Time Will Come

Life is like winter. Sometimes trials just like snow, keep pouring down. People hurt you, put you down; work is challenging, and it just seems as if you cant catch a break. But just as winter will give way for beautiful spring, you have to hold on to Gods promise and believe Him for a new season in your life as well. The sun will shine in your life again, and thats the truth. Beautiful people will come into your world, the ones God has sent to hold your hands will arrive soon. Business will blossom like beautiful roses, and you will find your voice again.

Just believe!

- February 26, 2015

Are You Listening? (1)

He speaks through the thick clouds that birth rain right when our soul gets thirsty,

He speaks through the actions of friends and foes that cause us pain that stabs our hearts,

He speaks through love, especially from sources we least expect,

He speaks through the loss of loved ones that take us on the ride of our lives,

He speaks in all the twists and turns of life,

Indeed, God speaks,

The real question is, Are You Listening?

- April 20th, 2015

Are You Listening? (2)

He speaks through verses in authentic scriptures,

He speaks through the miracles of life and death,

He speaks through the growth of plants and breaths of animals,

He speaks through lifes trials and triumphs,

No doubt He speaks,

The question is, Are you listening?

Tuesday, July 28th, 2015

Pray

Pray more when things are good; when your marriage is blissful, work is thriving, your kids are healthy and well behaved, and you are in good health.

Praying in good times is like storing water when its raining or saving when you are rich. There will be something to draw from when times get tough, and water to drink when there is a drought.

- July 30th, 2015

Handcuffs

They sat in dark smoke-
filled dark abroad
While their men seized
slaves in broad daylight.
They ruled and ruined
the fate of men far
away,
Then one day,
Songs of victory took over the airwaves,
But it wasnt over.
How foolish we were!
The metal chains may be gone,
But the men smoking cigars in dark rooms are alive,
And we are still enslaved,
Still trapped,
Just not with metal chains,
Now we are hooked to their gadgets.

- September 14th, 2015

Conquer

The only limitation you have is in your mind. Once you conquer your mind, you will conquer the world.

- December 13th, 2015

The Real Enemy

When its all said and done, the only enemy that keeps us down, blocks our progress, and hides our success is FEAR.

- January 8th, 2016

Love In Cancun Poems

Originally published on April 17, 2016

Your Mind

Your mind is the most powerful tool you own,
It is the inventor of your biggest miracles,
And the mother of your worst nightmare.
So, be protective of your thoughts,
Guard your dreams and possibilities,
And most of all, be mindful of who you allow to live rent-free in it.

Life

Dont measure your life by counting the days,

Measure it by the weight of your moments,

Not just the moments that take your breath away,

Or the ones that make your heart skip,

Measure your life by the moments you are present,

Each moment your heart shows up for is worth a lifetime.

Take a pause now and again,

To feel the magic in the swaying of the ocean,

The submission of the trees,

The victory of the sun despite dark clouds,

Then its own setting as decreed by its Lord.

And the gentle assurance in the moons appearance,

To feel the romance between the stars and the nights breeze.

When you find the magical moments,

Be present to capture them,

Not with gadgets crafted by men,

But simply with the perfect harmony within you,

The one between your eyes and the depths of your heart,

Then you will have captured them forever.

Do It

To capture a powerful moment forever, set your eyes on a blind date with your heart. To give life to your most beautiful dreams, create a lasting love affair between your pen and paper.

Ask Him

Remember your Lord always,
Ask of Him shamelessly,
Without reservations,
Or restrictions,
Ask from Him alone,
And have high expectations,
For He is the best compensator,
And the best compensation,
All in One.

The Race

The dead man is not the soulless case lying in a coffin,
The dead man is the breathing case who wastes his soul,
Running around the world with no dreams,
Having nothing to aspire to, but his sojourn in the grave.

Your Why

Would you sing a different song,
If you thought about the why?
Would you say another prayer,
If you didnt think about the what?
What exactly would you long for?
Hope for,
Wish for,
Cry for,
If you just take a moment,
To think about your why?

Seduction

You dont know what seduction is until you have seen the ocean;

Seduction is not a naked woman trying to lure her prey,

Seduction is the ocean at dawn when it wakes the palm trees

With its breeze, gently yet suggestively swaying ashore.

Seduction is the ocean in the still of the night

When it lures the walker with its sweet, beautiful lips,

With warm kisses on her feet urging her to let go.

Seduction is the warm embrace of the heart

Tight, yet not strong enough to choke.

Its the nod of acceptance of the palm trees

As though calling and urging in voices so low,

Yet the non-swimmer hears it louder than the mermaid.

Seduction is the art of temptation only the ocean has mastered.

Have You Ever?

Have you ever dared to pause,
To hear the sound most divine?
Have you ever stayed still,
To listen to the orchestra without a band?
Have you ever taken a moment,
To feel the miracle within your soul?
If you have never heard yourself breathe,
You have never heard the soundtrack of life.

I Found Love

Love for God, in spite of His Invisibility.

Love for my life, in spite of my flaws.

Love for the world, in spite of its turbulence.

Love for my purpose, in spite of its challenges.

Love for my inner circle, in spite of their imperfections.

Love for the ocean, in spite of my inabilities.

Indeed, I found love in Cancun.

On its beautiful beaches,

In its gentle breeze,

And especially its amazing souls,

In Rigo when he declared,

You make my day very happy.

And Carlos when he kept his promise to make coconut fritters on Friday,

In Juan when he greeted me with tea and mixed fruit juice every morning,

And in all the men and women who smiled, spoke, and nodded,

Through them all, I found love in Cancun.

Rain On The Beach

Have you ever watched the sky sing with the ocean?

Ever seen how they rave so loudly yet no one but them really feels the melody?

Ever watched them feed each other without a care in the world,

While glorifying the one who match-made them?

The sky praising the heavens with loud roars,

And the ocean prostrating and bowing in adoration in its rich turquoise splendor.

Then which of the favors of your Lord will you deny?

Storm Rider

Dont ask God to take the storms away; the storms will only stop when we die. Instead, tell Him to fortify your vessel with strength and light to help you ride and rise like the eagle.

- May 2nd, 2016

Soulmates

When I watched you breathe last night,
I saw your heart of gold,
Tucked firmly within your chest,
Beating sweetly to the rhythm of the night,
The peace on your divinely lit face,
In sync with the calmness of the moonlight,
You were miles away engrossed in your dreams,
Yet you moved my soul so powerfully.

So I obeyed,
Knelt right beside you,
And swayed to the rhythm of your heartbeat,
And just like the magical soundtrack of our lives,
Your dreams had me in them too,
I know because you smiled,
That gentle smile that melts my icy fears.
And our spirits vowed again,
That I will love you till eternity,
And you will love me forever plus one,
I know because we put the soul in a soul mate.

- May 15th, 2016

Act Like The Sun

When you dont feel like getting out of bed in the morning,

Act like the sun, which shows up for work no matter what.

When you feel unappreciated and ignored,

Act like the sun on winter days when no one notices its work.

When the storms of life threaten to drown out your efforts,

Act like the sun when it conquers dark clouds at dawn.

When the devil tries to sow seeds of pride in your heart,

Act like the sun, which shines its light equally on all.

When its time to walk, but cheers and fears hold you back,

Act like the sun that sets out each day, no matter who is watching.

- July 31st, 2016

Guard Your Wealth

Every moment you spend doing work that is not aligned with your purpose, or engaging people you are not supposed to serve, is priceless wealth lost, which you may never recover.

- October 26th, 2016

Don't

Dont count your losses,
Count the lessons.
Dont count your riches,
Count your blessings.
Dont stare at the calendar with anxiety,
Gaze at it with hope and expectations.
Expectations from the one who is the best compensator,
And the only compensation all in one.

- December 31st, 2016

If You Must

If you must bet,
Bet on you.
If you must follow,
Follow your dreams.
If you must compete,
Compete with you.
If you must fight,
Fight your fears.
If you must lose,
Lose the chains.
If you must stay,
Stay in action.
And if you must create,
Create a path.

- February 7th, 2017

Never End A Journey

Never end a journey,
Until you leave a piece of you.
Sow a seed,
And create a smile,
Fall in love,
And wipe a tear,
And when you wonder,
What to take back home,
Know that clothes fade,
And chocolates melt,
But the stories you tell
Of the moments your heart was there,
Will never be erased
From the hearts that hear.

- February 9th, 2017

A Beautiful Mind

Every soul needs a restful and safe place to go every day, and the best place is right inside of us a beautiful mind.

- February 11th, 2017

Winter Mornings

On those difficult days when you fall so short of your goals, as in, really miss the mark in spite of your best efforts, I hope you reflect on the fact that the success of the sun is not measured by the amount of heat we feel on windy winter mornings.

- February 11th, 2017

I Dare You

I dare you to dream so big,
Your heart begins to race.
I dare you to ask so boldly,
Your feet start to move.
I dare you to write down your prayers,
So your heart knows them by name.
I dare you to ask with no limits,
I dare you to shed the apparels of religion,
And clothe your soul with spirituality.
I dare you to leap without seeing the parachute.
What I am doing, my friend,
Is daring you to believe!

- February 18th, 2017

40 Things I Learned At 40

Originally Published On April 17th, 2017

1. Religion is a piece of clothing; it only makes a fashion statement when it adorns a spiritually connected heart.
2. Faith, like weight, is never constant.
3. The best way to supplicate is to connect with your GPS in the language you both understand.
4. I am not really afraid of dying; I am more fearful of not living.

5. The only reason you are still alive is because your mission is not yet complete; it has nothing to do with a special status.
6. The Almighty speaks; the question is, are you listening?
7. Dont get married because you are getting old and lonely. The misery of loneliness is nothing compared to the poison of a toxic marriage.
8. Getting married before understanding your mission is like getting into your car with a hitchhiker and driving around aimlessly for the rest of your life.
9. You cant serve from an empty cup. Prioritize frequent and meaningful self-care.
10. The loss of a parent is like losing a special light bulb thats been discontinued, but the loss of a child, born or unborn, is like a wound that never heals.
11. Death is not the only thing that ends relationships; some friendships end because, like viruses, they have run their course.
12. Be protective of your dreams. Some people are meant to be spectators in your arena, not strategists in your locker room.
13. Never start a marathon without your cheerleaders; they are the fuel you will need to finish the race strong.

14. Be wary of the Yes-ers, they are agents of failure.
15. Dont trust anyone who hardly sees the good in others.
16. Never compete; once you gain clarity on your why and your who, you will realize that no one else could have been sent to do your job.
17. Fall in love, but first with yourself in spite of your flaws, and then others.
18. I dont believe anyone who tells me they dont care what anyone thinks of them. We all need validation and approval; the key is choosing our audience carefully.
19. There is nothing wrong with failing and falling, but you have to check constantly that the person setting the passing grade is you.
20. Dont pick up phone calls of people who want to make their emergency your priority, and those who only get in touch when they need a favor.
21. You dont have to be an entrepreneur or social worker, as long as you are fully and wholly serving your tribe, you are honoring your calling.
22. The first time you think you have arrived is day one on the slippery slope to failure.
23. Financial success, to me, is living a simple and unpretentious life. I am okay as long as I climb into bed debt-free, even if my mattress is small.

24. Success happens if you are close to the door when opportunity knocks.

25. Dont teach what you arent constantly studying, and dont learn from someone who isnt a student.

26. You will never experience mind-blowing success if you arent ready to fail woefully.

27. Its okay to walk alone sometimes. You may be blazing a trail for an entire generation to follow.

28. There is no promotion without examination, no purpose without pain. Every scar and tear was designed to birth a new you.

29. On those hard days when your faith just wont overpower your fears, dont fight, dont feel guilty, just ask for the next day.

30. Fancy clothes and bright makeup cannot light up a dark soul.

31. Quit being the professional critic. You arent creating any joy if the only thing you see is what he or she did wrong.

32. The wise save and spend, while the foolish hoard and waste.

33. The best way to breathe life into your thoughts is to write them down.

34. Travel often, and travel alone, not only will your loved ones survive, they will appreciate the better you that emerges.

35. If your mind can conceive it, your Lord can do it.
36. Never want anything or anyone too much; you will end up crossing hard lines.
37. I strive to work harder than I did yesterday, but I choose up to 3 days every month when I do nothing but eat, sleep, and pray.
38. Forgive yourself again and again. Thats a prerequisite for forgiving others.
39. The only battles we win are the ones we walk away from before they even begin.
40. Do it afraid. Fly with your fear. If you wait for everything to fall into place before you leap, you will find yourself in your grave full of regrets.

Like It Depends On You

Pray like you arent working hard. Work like it depends on your efforts alone. And most importantly, hope like your entire life depends on it. The muscles you build during this struggle will help you survive when you achieve what you seek.

- April 30th, 2017

May Your Soul See

May your soul see;
Ease in every difficulty,
Victory in every defeat,
Success in every failure,
Gain in every loss,
And Purpose in every pain.
May your soul see;
Opportunities in every challenge.

- June 6th, 2017
Dedicated to the Grand Rapids City High School Class of 2017.

The Miracle

The miracle isnt your GPS taking you where you want to go; the real miracle is your GPS taking you exactly where you need to be.

- August 7th, 2017
Inspired by Quran 1:6

You Can

When you are tired and cant go on,
Take another step.
When your heart feels too weary and disconnected,
Hope for something big.
When you dont know how to fund that huge dream,
Sow the most generous seed.
When you think it is not enough,
Give the almighty thanks for it.
When your levies are completely broken,
Like there is no single fight left in you,
Close your eyes and take a leap.
The worst that can happen is a fall,
But you will never crash.
Your GPS will always be there to rescue you.
This struggle is for a reason:
To birth a new you.
But do it now
Because you can!

- September 17th, 2017

Count Your Losses

They always say to count your blessings,

But not today.

Today, I want you to count your losses,

Yes, losses!

I am talking about the pains, obstacles, and difficulties,

Count them and see them.

Cant you see

The loss of wealth that made you thrifty?

The loss of status that made you humble?

The loss of freedom that gave you focus?

The pain of sickness that made you spiritual?

The loss of life that made you present?

The pain of betrayal that gave you freedom?

The loss of relationships that gifted you purpose?

And the heartbreak that made you stronger?

For indeed, With every difficulty, there is ease.

- October 5th, 2017

How Can?

How can you call it a victory if it doesnt have a story?

How can you give God the glory, if you never had to worry?

- October 10th, 2017

Hurricane

Trials are like hurricanes,
They come in categories,
And storm in seasons.
Some so strong,
They knock out power from your soul,
Others so weak.
All they do is rain on your spirit.
No matter what category your hurricane is,
Regardless of how much wind it packs on its back,
Know that your recovery will happen;
Not just because you were prepared,
And that your power will be restored,
Not because of your strength,
Know that help will come,
Not just because you got a crew of first responders,
Know that mountains will move and paths will open,
Because you are connected to the GPS that never fails.

- October 13th, 2017

God

God is the light that brightens the dark alley,
The outlet at the dead end,
The hope in the hopeless case,
The rescue when the parachute fails,
And the solution when the formula breaks.

When there is no other place to go,
And nothing else works,
When the case becomes hopeless,
And everyone helpless,
Its at that spot,
In that space,
And at that time,
You see God in His full majesty.

- October 21st, 2017
Inspired by Quran 2:186

Man

Look at man,
Afraid to spend for fear of poverty,
To eat for fear of hunger,
Scared to sleep for fear of lateness,
To love for fear of heartbreak.
Afraid to dance for fear of ridicule,
To strive for fear of failure,
Scared to walk for fear of falling.
Just look at him,
He thinks he is afraid of dying,
When the only thing that scares the life out of him is living.

- October 24th, 2017

Dust And Ashes

Look at man,
Marching proudly,
Screaming loudly,
And raising his shoulders
Because he is on the earth.

Does he not know,
That he is one bill away from poverty?
One call away from calamity,
One cough away from sickness,
Or one step away from death?

Look at man,
Marching proudly,
Screaming loudly,
And raising his shoulders
Because he forgets;
The only thing thats sure
Is that soon,
He will soon be in the earth.

- November 1st, 2017

Space Holder?

What are you?
And what do you have?
A spouse or a space-holder?
A spouse furthers,
A space-holder hinders.
A spouse rocks,
A space-holder blocks.
A spouse stays through it all,
A space-holder stays till the tides turn.

You think a space-holder is till you find better, because you deserve better, so he/she is just temporary, but thats a big lie because the damage to your soul is permanent. The worst relationship is where one thinks he/she is a spouse, but is in reality, just a space-holder.

So again, I ask: What are you? What do you have?

- December 7, 2017

Lean In

When you are too tired to run, lean in.

When you are too weak to walk, lean in.

When you think you cant go on, lean in.

Lean in when your legs just wont move.

Close your eyes,

Lean in to your spirit,

And let the good winds take over,

They somehow know exactly where you are meant to be.

- December 7th, 2017

Hijab

It bothers you,
Offends you,
Unsettles you,
And even annoys you.
But I dont know why.

You trivialize it,
Abuse it,
Call it a mere cloth,
You even call me stupid,
And I dont know why.

Did you know?
It is my honor,
My identity,
My obedience,
My ticket,
My cover,
My dignity?
Did you?

Wait,

Listen,

Sir, would you strip off your underpants for a quick shot?

Miss, could you lift up your shirt for a quick minute?

Yes, here, right here, now.

Tough? Okay.

Would you mind strolling down the road naked then?

Oh, you are asking me why?

I will tell you

Right after you help me understand.

How come my hijab hurts you?

- December 20th, 2017

Your Troops

Never leave home without your troops;
The cheerleaders,
Louder than naysayers,
Quieter than truth tellers,
And more present than Yes-Men.

Dont forget your mentors,
Your band of believers,
And an army of pushers,
You will need them to get past the hilly exit.

- December 31st, 2017

Built To Inspire

You were made to rise;

Higher than the clouds,

Stronger than the elements,

And bigger than your struggles,

Like the eagle,

And the airplane,

Were built to fly,

You were made to soar,

You,

Yes, you,

Were built to inspire.

- January 1st, 2018

No Break To Cry

There are times we suffer the hardest, most painful falls in our pursuit of happiness, yet we cant pause to cry. We see the bruises, yet we cant take a break to wail. So a trophy got away today, but if we dont get up and keep running despite the pain, we wont even appear in the tournament photos.

- January 9th, 2018

Inspire

Dont ask people to change, inspire them to act in their own best interests by living your truth, and sharing only that which nourishes their soul.

- January 11th, 2018

Yinka

We are the trees in the forest zoned for houses,

The sheep in the slaughter kept for parties,

We are the inmates in the section destined for the squad.

The exit schedule is unknown,
But our faith is sealed,
No room for appeals,
No option of parole,
We are the dead mourning the dead.

The strong tree grants shade with passion,
The good sheep gives meat with juice,
And the wise inmate lights up cells with melody.

For they know,
Like they know,
That their turn on the block is sure,

They will never be ready,

But their tongues will testify,

The earth will confirm,

And the angels will bear witness,

That they lived on purpose,

Loved with passion,

Left their imprints,

And so their mission was accomplished.

- February 2nd, 2018.
Dedicated to my friend,
Late Kifayah Yinka Ayo-Adeyemi

The Scope

Your only duty is to light up the world. No, you arent supposed to be the sole supplier of power; you are just required to let the light within you shine through.

- February 6th, 2018

A Prayer

Lord, grant me
The strength to believe,
So that I may ask,
And the power to be still,
So that I may listen,
Then the wisdom to trust,
So that I may wait.
Amin.

- February 7th, 2018

As- Salam Alaekum

Today, I wish you light. The sort that shines brightly into your soul, so you know you are strong enough to say NO to the work or relationship that doesnt serve your souls simple needs - to eat, sleep, and breathe well. But first, I wish you peace so you can see that light. As-salam Alaekum.

- February 12th, 2018

Be Your Valentine

The most important love affair is the one you have with you,

Dont wait for someone to love you,

And dont wait for a day to express that love.

Do it every day your failings stare back at you in the mirror.

Do it every time you hear the soundtrack of life in your lungs.

- February 14th, 2018

Miracle

A miracle is what happens when preparation meets answered prayers.

February 26, 2018

Yet You Rise!

You have to know that as long as the sun rises in spite of the dark clouds every morning, your breakthrough will come in spite of the struggles and challenges on your path now.

February 28, 2018

Ride

Life is not about how early you begin, or how well you end, it is not even about how well you ride. The essence of life is how well your tribe is served while you are on your journey.

- March 8, 2018

Past

The past can either be a parachute or an obstacle to a better future.

- March 9, 2018

Unplug

How will you hear from God when you are afraid to hear from you?

How will you hear the call when you are too scared to be alone?

March 10, 2018

Marriage

Marriage is one of the most important relationships you will ever form with another human being, so you must never settle. Settling isnt marrying someone on a lower level on the educational or socio-economic ladder. It is marrying someone with poorer values, character and integrity.

- March 11, 2018

So, which of the favors of your Lord will you deny?

- Quran 55